Complicated Simplicities

Jameel Watson

1.4.3

Being Remembered Is Essentially Love Lost Eventually

TABLE OF CONTENTS

...

Maybe I'm just a concept. A concept waiting to be understood. Something that can be mentally grasped, but not physically obtained. Well, I can be obtained, but at what cost to your emotional and mental health? Maybe I'm better off being thought of than had. Is it weird that I think I'm more valued as an idea more than a being? But why an idea? Why devalue myself to just a thought? I have to mean more than that. I hate self-reflecting. It gets scary at times. Seeing your thoughts on paper can be a frightening sight. Living with them is one thing, due to eventually becoming immune to them. It's when they're on display that bothers you. Once you put yourself out there, you're susceptible to criticism. That's why I'm scared to write sometimes. I scare myself, so imagine how the women I hurt feel. But I hate talking about my problems; I rather cause them.

STAGE 1

I always thought I could control my woman. In a mental fashion though, not in the aggressive do as I say or else style. That was too easy, and I didn't find much fun in that kind of manipulation. Damaging a woman's psyche while also momentarily deterring their progression without any physical contact was my style. It took a certain skill to accomplish this. It was art in a way. You have to appreciate art, right? I felt like every portrait of mine was a masterpiece, regardless of how my muse felt. Regardless of how taxing I was on their mental health. How can you tell a painter that his creation isn't valuable and worthy of acclaim? You can't.

The Art of Manipulation. That's probably what I'd call my course. I would have students filling the seats in my classroom trying to figure out how to get into the psyche of women.

I can envision the questions now. "How do you manage to have multiple women at one time?". "How do you put truths in your lies?". "Why do I let all the good women go, but keep the females that don't do as much as them around?" It would be hilarious. But most importantly, I would have every answer.

Relationships don't work if she isn't the girlfriend before you're the boyfriend. I feel like that's one of the components to longevity. You would be naive to believe both parties commit simultaneously. Relationships only work when the man likes the woman more than she likes him. Women love reassurance, so when that type of affection and attention is shown, they tend to commit mentally before coming to an agreement with the man verbally. There's nothing funnier than waking up to a relationship you didn't know you were in. It's kind of dope when you think about it. There's nothing better than a woman that commits to you before making you aware about it. I'd be lying to you if I said I believed that. The only thing better than that, is making her believe you're the boyfriend with no intent on being there for her as much as she's there for you. That's the best.

It's always impressive when you can create a vision you don't intend on championing but making it believable enough so that someone else could see it more clearly than you. That's when you know you're talented. I loved the fact that I was able to accomplish this with every woman that had faith in me. I guess I'm partially the blame for the blind faith instilled. But who cares? As long as I wasn't the one being misled, nothing bothered me.

I'm always asked, "why are you like this?" Besides "asking me if I'm hungry, that might be my favorite question to get asked. I don't care about the heartbreak or regression I cause. My ideologies are not meant to prevent that; it advocates for it. I'm more concerned with the person that blossoms from the psychological impediments placed upon them. I know causing distortion and manipulating a woman to make her better in the long run seems paradoxical, but that's just how it goes. Everyone has their strategies on how to make someone a better person. This just happened to be mine.

I can see all the students now; anxious to leave my class and go home to tell their friends and family about the lecture I just gave. Rushing to pull out their devices to tweet and post quotes from my soliloquy. I hope they credit me. I hate when you initiate an idea and other people run with it as their own. But anyway, I hope that all the students could learn all my techniques. I wish I could train them individually, so that they can be just as precise as me. I would hate to be the catalyst of a failed system. There just might be a place for me in society that enables me to be myself. Maybe my mother was right.

I wish people understood that this is a craft. A craft I take extremely seriously. I pride myself on being a thinker, so I focused on the psyche of women. Knowing that I could embed certain behaviors in a woman's mind and break her down mentally and emotionally fed my ego. I found so much joy in that. I did it so often that it became routine; natural in a way. You know when something is routine, it's easy for you to internalize it as a natural act. That's the scary part; thinking abnormal behavior is a normality. I see nothing wrong with my actions or train of thought.

I don't know where people came up with the idea that everyone is supposed to treat everybody with the best intentions. It never really works out that way. There's always a culprit and a victim. But it's comical in a way; going through life not expecting to get used. Life taught me that everyone is an instrument- You use them to your advantage. If you can't be used, then you're useless, right? I would rather be utilized as someone's means to better themselves, opposed to being looked at as someone who serves no purpose. But whatever.

My goal wasn't to hurt women, but to feed my vices. In my corrupted mind, it seemed as though they went hand in hand. I hate the word corrupt. The meaning of that word seemed to carry a negative connotation. As if I'm morally depraved or something. As if my behavior and cognitive transgressions weren't the standard or normal behavior that gets exhibited by everyone on a day to day basis. Or maybe it doesn't. It could just be me and a select few that harness this gift. I'm probably not too fond of the word 'corrupt' because it fit me so well. I don't know… maybe disrupting the mental of women was my vice.

I loved putting women in positions where I was the one who dictated the outcome. Everything goes through me. How you talk, who you interact with, who your new friends will be; I needed to be in control of that. As my woman, aren't you supposed to trust my judgment? Aren't you supposed to be submissive and do everything that makes the relationship better, even if it's to your own detriment? I thought women liked men who took initiative. I thought women liked when men who are assertive. I thought women like men who has a clear understanding of they are. I rather be this guy, than the one who gets walked over due to not stepping up. That couldn't be me. I love stepping up, even if my woman suffered the consequences. I wish this type of control wasn't so easy employ. Maybe I'd be a better man.

It's fucked up that this mindset is carried out amongst individuals, but with certain demons, you must learn to embrace them instead of trying to alter. I am my demons. I would look at myself in a weird light if I ever chose to shelf that side of me, just to create a better image for someone else. Corruption is a prerequisite to progression. Why turn down or hide the gift that God ultimately gave me?

I wish I could talk to him. I'm interested to know his opinion on how I carry myself. I doubt he'll be receptive on that conversation. I speak to him all the time, but he doesn't say anything back. I don't know how I feel about that. Do you see the position that puts me in? I now have to make these decisions with no guidance. Now I have to be responsible for someone else's feelings. I can't be held accountable if I don't receive help, right? But I learned that I have to stop doing that. I have a habit of using greater forces to justify my actions. To justify why I lack accountability for my actions. Plus, that's a scary game to play; using God as an excuse to behave in the manner that I do. But, I played the game so well. I infiltrated so well. I made women second guess their woman's intuition so well. And honestly, I found my peace with this. I mastered this. I just wish people understood me. That's all.

I always resented the friends of the women I dated. They complicated the whole process. Once you exude certain attributes and embed your ideologies in your woman, the only people that notice what you're doing are her friends. I swear it seems like once you're involved with a woman, you're dating her friends as well. It's weird.

If you go out and her friends happen to see you, more than likely, they're giving your woman a progress report of what you're doing. You can't even be seen with another woman while the friends are around. I wonder why the friends never exhausted that much energy into their own relationships. It's never her productive friends with the relationship, car, job and own place that do all the extra investigation. It's the single, can't keep a man to sit still- friends, who do all the research. Why can't they keep a man? Is it that challenging? Clearly, it must be since being single is an epidemic now. I Just hate intrusive friends who never seem to have business of their own. It's clear I'm not too fond of the friends my women have.

I always thought that after a certain age, being single is a disability. I envision some type of agent or social worker coming to your home and doing some sort of intervention to figure out the problem. The government giving out stipends to people who are alone. That's how I see it coming about. Life isn't constructed for single people. Life is made for cohabitation and compromise, not single-person experiences.

Yeah, you can eat dinner at a restaurant by yourself, but the waiter or waitress has to come over and remove that other seat from the table. The only thing worse than being single for an extended period of time, is getting accustomed to it. Once you get comfortable with the idea of seclusion, the purpose of life has officially escaped you. I don't know, I could be wrong. Although I believe life is made for cohabitation and compromise, I think people simplify it to cohabitation and temptation; which might make more sense depending on who you're asking. The more you gravitate towards one, the more you divert yourself away from the other. Then again, I don't know. I hate when I'm uncertain about my own philosophies. I'm not sure if I'm pro relationships or not. I do believe that most geniuses and creators produce their best work when they aren't involved with someone. Relationships dilute creativity. So maybe I am against it. But it's whatever. I hate getting off topic.

I wonder if the friends of the woman you date intrude so much because they have too much time on their hands and they want to make themselves seem useful? I always had the idea that the more her friends tried to invade, the more jealous they were. Why else are they so adamant in their pursuit to find the wrongs in their friend's relationship? Even if their friend is dealing with an asshole; that's none of their business. At all. What benefit do they get from that? I never understood that. Sometimes you have to let your friend look like a dumbass when it comes to the man they're entertaining. Shielding them doesn't aid in progression. People undervalue the power of pain and anguish. Everyone should be a product of relationship agony. I'm tired of encountering men and women walking around without any type of suffrage that derived from prior relationships. Why haven't you've been heartbroken yet? Why arc you so confident that you'll find someone who makes you happy? I can't stand happy people. But then again, I guess that's what friends are supposed to do. But it's funny because the friends of the women I dated made it so much easier for me to manipulate and control them.

It appeared that the more they tried to tell my woman how corrupt I was, the more my woman gravitated towards me. As she should. As every woman should. If the opinions from her friends causes for your woman to depart from you, your woman's intent to be with you was never genuine. No one can make your woman leave you, but you. But I guess I could thank and credit them for why I'm like this. It's kind of weird because the friends were so against me that it kind of turned me on. Not in a sexual way or anything, but mentally. I felt challenged; disrespected in a way. They were chiming in on our relationship and hinting that their friend should leave me alone, as if I wouldn't do the same thing to them if they were mine. I'm that skilled. I often wanted to take that risk. Typically, when your woman brags about you to her friends, the friends then become curious; wanting to know or experience it firsthand. Every woman needs their curiosity stroked.

Women really have to keep an eye on their friends. That friend that get that extra laugh out when your man tells a joke. That friend that hugs your man a second too long. That friend whose conversation dims when you tell them good news about your relationship.

It's fucked up that women can't even tell their friends how good their man is without one of them wanting to find out for themselves. Friends don't really be friends; especially when you're enjoying things they never could. I wish more women knew that. I'm glad I knew how to pick them. But yeah, no woman is above my system. The same way I had my lady, I would've had their friends in the same position. Any position; and you can take that however you want. This is what I practiced. This is my craft. If only they knew.

I think I mostly resented the friends because they never let me control my woman and execute my plan in peace. I guess that's admirable. Doing what they think is the right thing to do to protect their so-called friend. It's cute I guess. I always found a way, though. I was meticulous and methodical in the way I approached this course of action. I had a fascination with damaged women. When I refer to damaged women, I'm alluding to women that need rehabilitation. Women that have been repeatedly hurt by men, but always give the next one the benefit of the doubt. The females that been through a lot with guys that never seemed to peak as high as them.

I was that guy that never peaked. I was the benefit
of the doubt guy that was never deserving of the
benefit. Although on most occasions I wasn't
worthy of the benefit, I always found a way to
make women believe I warranted that treatment. I
was disingenuous with a lot of my actions; doing
things that seemed good natured, just to reap the
advantages of doing so. I love the ability that
women have to work with a man. I just hated that
they were gullible enough to work with one that
never showed progression. You see why I love
damaged women? I've observed that women who
have been hurt one too many times, love harder. I
think that's a natural coping mechanism for them.
They give the next man more of them in hopes of
the effort being reciprocated, opposed to giving
the next man a hard time because of what they
endured before him. There's nothing worse than a
woman that makes a man pay for another man's
mistakes. Being able to offer more of yourself
after a failed attempt is a special attribute. I know
if I were in situations that repeatedly caused me
distress and led to my feelings being manipulated,
I wouldn't be as open to dealing with new people.

I always wondered what having feelings felt like. I understand it as it relates to family. That's unconditional and almost everyone experiences that. But intimately, I was always curious. I've witnessed the effect it has on people and always wanted to know where it derived from. What's the process? Is it something that's controllable? From the outside looking in, it seems complicated. I always thanked God for not allowing me to have to deal with this dilemma. I guess he does speak to me. Maybe that's why I gravitated towards damaged women. The love they were willing to give out to any guy who possessed attractive attributes would garner any man's attention. It's sad that I take advantage of these women. What's worse, is that they allow me to.

My mom is an amazing woman. The beauty and value I see in that woman is insurmountable. Maybe she's where I got the idea of a damaged woman. It never crossed my mind until I picked up this pen. My mom wasn't as fortunate as some women as it relates to their quest in finding one man and living her life happily. She didn't deal with an abundance of men, but the ones she did deal with never seemed to put her in high spirits.

I never payed attention to it until now. What's wrong with my mom? She made something out of nothing- every time. I don't know how she does it. Have you ever witnessed your mother make miracles out of misfortunes? It takes a special woman to do that. With those types of qualities, I would expect a man to realize that she's a blessing. To understand that she's rare. I guess it's natural for a son to wish their mom happiness in all forms. At the same time though, the only unconditional love she needs is from my siblings and I, right? What does she need anybody else for?

Although I hated seeing my mom lonely, I didn't aid in the process of her keeping a man. I was never an advocate of her bringing a man around the house. It just didn't sit right with me. I never seen her progress after dealing with guys. Isn't that their job? To make you better? Even if the relationship didn't go as planned, your job is to make sure that she didn't leave the relationship with the same type of thinking and knowledge that she came into it with. At the bare minimum, that's your job as a man. There was this one guy I was fond of her dealing with, but you know how that story goes.

I wouldn't be speaking of my mom if that worked out. As I got older and started to realize she's not getting any younger, I figured she has to have a life as well. Her kids can't be her comfort forever. I just hated the guys she dealt with. And they were always shorter than me. Women really like short men? Dos that make them feel superior? I think that's probably the real reason why I never liked the men she thought about entertaining. If they were out and something were to have happened, I get a visual of him looking up at her waiting for her to find a solution. She could do better.

All I knew was my dad; the little of him that was around. The typical black boy story. I really don't want to talk about this man. I think the meaning of that word needs to be altered. That's a privilege to have that title of a man in my opinion. I'm all for that movement. Whenever he did come around, he left right back. He never stayed to see how I turned out. I know I wasn't the best son, but damn. Whenever he's the topic, I always find a way to blame myself for his actions. Why do I always take the blame for trying to fill the void of a missing figure? Thinking about him always put me in an uncomfortable state.

He hasn't even done enough to be thought of. I always wanted to see what the finished product of me would've been like if he would've held his ground. I hate talking about this. Emotions consistently find a way to cloud my judgment. It makes me seem human. I hate seeming human. It implies you can get hurt, and I am definitely not a proponent of that. It's funny how I don't condone his actions from a son's standpoint, but I exhibit these same behaviors when dealing with women. I wonder if he plays a part in why I act and think the way I do now, as far as leaving and not caring about how I impacted women. Why couldn't he have just stayed? But that's another story. I really like to call that my mother's story.

But back to her. As an observer, I can tell that she's been through a lot. It's funny because I have all the emotion and feelings in the world as it pertains to my mom, but treat other women that I feel as though have the same qualities, in a different manner. Maybe if I didn't view women as a condition, I wouldn't have this complex. The more I pondered on it, the more I realized that I actually turned into the exact guys I have seen fail her. That didn't hit me until I put down my pen.

Long live the man who sacrifices his vices. I wish this was applicable to me. Although I witnessed the pain my mom wears on her sleeve from guys like me, I still chose to take advantage of women. And I loved it. The process was simple. I showed false potential. Women love false potential. You display it, and here they go thinking you're different than the rest of the guys they've encountered. I hate that women are so gullible when they're in a vulnerable position. Then again, no I don't. I really should stop that. I make people think I actually care, when in all reality, these are the same circumstances in which I thrive in. If they're gullible, it makes the deceit that much easier. I acknowledge how unpleasant this sounds. It gives me a misogynistic feel. But I don't care. Who said that all potential is beneficial? Potential is just having or showing the capacity to become or develop into something in the future. Having the capacity to accomplish something, doesn't guarantee anything. It's just hope you see in someone or something that could possibly manifest into greatness or productivity. The more you've been through with people who've disappointed you, the more lenient you'll be with someone who crosses your path and exhibits a glimpse of upside.

At least that's how I think the story goes. You give chances to those who give you a reason to.

I loved giving false hope. But then again, who doesn't? It's a game everyone plays. It's enticing. Everyone just has their own technique about how they go about it; but everyone indulges. The only people who are opposed to this, are the ones who failed and aren't as adept at playing this game. I made every girl feel as though they were the only woman I was dealing with. I used to be the guy that gave every girl the same conversation. Why waste them? I made all of them feel like they were wanted. It was an arduous task keeping up with each of their likes and dislikes. There was so much I had to remember. I had notebooks and shit, reminding me of what I said to each woman and the strategies I planned on implementing to get them to care more than they could afford to. It was a game to me; seeing who would fall for what or how long I could keep every interest interested. And as soon as I started to feel as though one was getting tired of my bullshit, she became the priority of the non-important. That's generally how it went. It was a list.

Whoever I sensed was closest to moving on to a man that deserved them, received the most attention. Once I have your attention, you cannot leave under your own conditions. I had to decide departure times. The ones I knew that weren't going anywhere, stayed at the bottom of the list. You know how that goes. I'm sure you can relate. I get mad when people pretend as if they do not understand this system. You keep people around until they realize their worth is more important than the situation you put them in. Why go to someone who could treat you better when you have me? I never understood why they would do that. I wish more people stood up and admitted that they share the same views so that I wouldn't be the only one seen as a psychological abuser.

Eventually, you just say fuck it and embrace your behaviors. I wish there was a facility that housed people of my kind; an isolated establishment where nobody knows us but us. We could be ourselves and not have to fit in with the regular people. I never understood regular people. That whole taking into account of other people's feelings when you do certain things. I wasn't with it. How could I be? Doesn't that get in the way of what you're trying to accomplish?

That couldn't be me. If I cared about how you would react to my thinking, it would impede everything that I'm trying to do in life.

I hated that I was so arrogant in my way of thinking. I never made time to equate people's problems to mine. Our dilemmas could never compare. People deal with relationship problems and wonder why their partner doesn't show them enough attention. Or how come they can never be in a relationship with someone who cares as much as they do. Or they worry about if their partner is being loyal when they aren't around. I have a different set of problems. Problems that include me wondering why the psyche of this woman is stronger than I intended, forcing me to utilize other measures of manipulation. I have to figure out how I'm going to play mind games with some lady's daughter and at the same time get the father's approval of me. You see the facade I have to put on? Those are real problems. Not wondering if your partner is texting somebody at night in the same bed that you both share. People need to understand that there's logic behind manipulation and mind games. It builds character for the long run. I hate encountering weak psyches.

The type of people who never got fucked over and are so positive in life.

It might be hard to believe, but I do this for the betterment of women. I love women. The psychological damage I do impose is all for a greater purpose. I'm all for the restoration of females. Sometimes you have to knock down an establishment and rebuild it for it to become stronger. I was great at that. Knocking down a wall, taking weeks and months to construct a new one. Emptying out her literary bank and supplying her with a brand-new shipment of words. Remodeling old philosophies of theirs and making it easier for men like me to get their attention. There's multiple routes to progression. I chose to inflict distortion and psychological agony before I made them a product of development.

I'm starting to realize that my role just might be to make the person I'm dealing with better for the next person they entertain. Everyone can't be the long-term person. The same way you have to make sacrifices in a relationship, people have to learn to be sacrifices themselves.

It's a shitty role sometimes because every now and then I feel like that's all it'll ever be. I'll encounter someone and establish a bond with them for a few months and then I'll be on my way. And she'll be with her new man, while he benefits from everything I instilled in her. I get jealous of that sometimes. This is one of those times when being regular would help. I wanted to stay on a few occasions and see what I helped reconstruct. For some reason I never stayed around long enough to witness the benefits of my tactics or the pain I inflicted.

Damn, I hate my father. Was that his purpose? To leave and make me stronger in the process? Did he believe that life had a better chance of raising me than he did? I hate making excuses for this character. And I hate how his absence is playing such a relevant role in my life today. He doesn't deserve that.

I wonder what would it take to actually build that facility that housed people of the mentally depraved. What activities would be conducted in there? I couldn't imagine the relationships. It would probably be one big ass game of chess. Knowing that everyone in there has a hidden agenda and can't be detected because everyone has an eclectic way of thinking. It's funny in a way because you wouldn't be able to trust anyone. You would second guess everyone's intentions. But as far as judgment, there would be none. You could interact freely and not have to put on a facade for the regulars. I wonder if they could adjust to our realm. Just imagine them having to accommodate to us. It would be funny seeing them try and be psychological abusers. I wish I could pull up a chair and watch it in action. I would pay anything to see this transpire. I wonder how their mannerism would alter knowing that everyone there thinks and moves completely different. I'm sure they wouldn't be comfortable. That's why I hate when I try to explain my condition to people and they look at me like I'm wrong for behaving the way I do. I find comfort in distortion. They wouldn't last one fucking day in there. All the condemning that comes with this identity would be normalized.

I hate getting agitated as I write. The real me always finds a way to show itself. I try to refrain from letting it take over for the purpose of me getting my message across to the readers appropriately but it's extremely difficult. We all get mad when we are misunderstood. I think that's one of the only things that connects everyone in this world. It doesn't matter what language you speak, what religion you practice, what mental illness one might possess, we can all relate to being misunderstood. Nobody is fond of that. How you perceive something could be so simple, but since it's foreign to them or too abstract, people don't see your vision. That's why I wish this facility existed. I wouldn't have these issues. We would all be understood in a weird psychological way. We would understand that the differences in the way we infiltrate minds is what ultimately unites us. It's crazy how unity forms.

I always wanted to pick up new tactics, though. There must be a million and one ways to infiltrate the mind and cause distress and-or promote rehabilitation. I'd just sit back and write down all the techniques they talked about while I kept mine to myself. I'm too arrogant and proud of what I've invented to share with anybody.

But you'd think that since I was so proud of my abilities, I'd be willing to share my techniques, right? I would just hate to be outdone. I'm a man with pride, so I couldn't risk hearing other people's tactics just to realize that I'm nowhere on their level. They'd probably be telling me their best shit, too. How they said this and made their partner do that. How they consciously instilled certain behaviors and mannerisms in their partner, which led to them having the upper hand. They probably would have some good shit. If only you could see the excitement on my face while writing this. The freedom this would give me. But unfortunately, life doesn't work that way. I hate coming back to reality.

One technique I mastered and started utilizing more is making women believe there's more to me than there really is. It might be my favorite game to play. I feel like I'm giving you too much of my world. Telling you all things that you don't deserve to know. This is sacred to me. It took a long time to build this. I don't like sharing, especially if the audience isn't appreciative of what I'm divulging. But then again, I guess that's the goal, right? To recruit. This life is way more interesting.

I got a habit of getting excited and diverting from my original thought when the prospect of getting people to cross over comes up. But I loved making women believe I offered more than I actually did. I only did this because I knew the habits of damaged women. For some reason, they have a knack for rehabilitating worthy men. Too bad I wasn't one of them. That's one thing I love about women; the ability to see a man and have the capability to get them off their feet and turn him into something. I was fully aware that took a special gift. It's fucked up that their talents go to waste by trying to fix me. That time and energy could've been exerted somewhere else; possibly to a man that's deserving. I needed no fixing. I knew exactly what to do and what behavior to convey to be a good man to someone. I just found no fun in that. Eventually you have to be a man and stop having fun and make grown decisions, right? I hear that all the time. These are the times you're supposed to enjoy. You're supposed to mishandle good people. You're supposed to treat a good woman like she ain't shit and deal with the consequences of seeing her with a man that'll do better. These are the times. Every man needs to experience losing the woman they always wanted. If a man never lost a good woman, he isn't ready for a serious relationship.

Every man has to endure this. How a man recovers from losing a worthy woman shows you his true character. It's hard to identify the true essence of a man if he never had to overcome this hardship.

Seeing young people settle is so upsetting. You are between the ages of 18 and 24, and you want to spend the rest of your life attached to one person? You don't even know what life is yet. How could you? But then again, I guess that's good. I wish my mom and father would have done that. I hate that I resemble him so much.

But I admire how a woman can turn a man's life around by just standing by his side and holding him down. I wonder where they learned that ability to rehabilitate men. How do they decipher through all the wolves in sheep's clothing and determine who's worth the effort? I wish I could get into their minds sometimes and learn that process. I want to know if I were them and I encountered me, would I notice? If I was in their position, would I be able to tell? I would hope not. I spent a great number of years perfecting this, so to be able to be easily spotted as a psychological abuser demotes my work.

Then again, it's kind of hard to be pointed out as one solely using the visual. You would actually have to get to know me. That's what I love about being this way. There's no physical traits that can help you pick me out of a lineup as someone who could manipulate you. I hate the portrait I paint of myself sometimes because I tend to paint too accurate of a picture. But I really am a good man, honestly. But that's what they all say. I embody everything that's needed. There's some women you can't persuade so I'm not even going to attempt to. And I hate sounding like the typical male, but my pride just won't enable me to be a good man even though I harness the necessary attributes to be one. I'm sure you all are curious as to what my meaning of a good man comprises of, due to how I depicted myself already. I'm sure I didn't create the best visual of myself. I really don't care though; this is me. But I don't think it's as difficult as women make it seem. I was always a provider. My favorite question to ask was "are you hungry?" A fed girlfriend is a faithful girlfriend. I don't recall ever encountering a woman that responded with 'no' when asked if they were hungry. Even if they are full, they'll always find a way to make use for it.

It's funny because food actually solves a lot of relationship issues. Has your girlfriend ever developed a bad attitude, but you don't know what you did to contribute to it? Then after you feed her, she's back to normal? Women are funny like that.

Now that I think about it, a fed girlfriend isn't a faithful girlfriend. Nothing you do can make a woman remain loyal; which is fucked up. You could be the perfect gentleman, but if she come across a man that strokes her curiosity, she's liable to indulge. Women's relationship status is contingent upon who you are. If you're attractive or prospering, she's single for you, even if she has a boyfriend. It's funny the things women condemn men for but do as well. But whatever. Isn't it interesting how women use sex? The man she likes and wants to keep around for the long run, has to wait to receive it. But the guy she's just psychically attracted to could get it whenever the opportunity arises. Obviously, women wouldn't blatantly admit it, but I know how they move. Nowadays, you just have to pray and hope you have a good person and remain loyal. Even if it doesn't work out, they could never say you didn't do your job.

What's the point of being a good man if your behavior doesn't dictate how she maneuvers? Sometimes, it's better to just be than man she likes, opposed to a good man. Because if she doesn't like you, what's the point?

But I offered more than food. The kisses on the forehead, nose, neck, between the breast, stomach and the inner thighs. I knew how to work women. It's the small details like that, that keeps them around. What does any of that have to do with being a good man, right? Every action counts. You'd be a fool to believe that women don't want their man to exhibit that behavior. I was also an advocate for encouraging my woman to do whatever satisfied her; as long as it didn't interfere with the disturbance I would eventually cause her. But of course, I couldn't make it obvious. You can't do shit like that. So, I just continued playing the cheerleader until I devised a new plan. It was actually cute though; watching my woman get her life together and enjoy herself, not even knowing I had other plans for her. It really does seem like I'm not pro my woman, but I am. Her happiness just has to derive from me. Any other source of fulfillment didn't sit well with me. Intellectually, I had the package as well. It's probably my best asset; being able to articulate my stances appropriately and make abstract conclusions. But I hated how easy it was to get women's attention with certain conversations. I guess that applies to everyone. It's funny how women react to words and ideologies they never heard before.

It really catches their eye. When you offer more than the "what you are doing?" conversation via text every two hours of the day, they take note. I always hated receiving them texts. Really? That's the only conversation you can offer as an adult? It's crazy the lack of substance people have in their dialogue.

But nonetheless, I had a system I've built for years. Nothing in that system called for me to exhibit the qualities of being a good man. And I always get asked what's the definition of a good man and I feel like I give a different meaning every time. A good man doesn't have to be a good man all the time, just when he needs to be. I was always great at picking the right time to show productivity. But I honestly believe it alters whenever you encounter a woman. What might be good to one woman, might be regular for the next. It's hard to speak on behalf of others because I know what I am, regardless of the portrait I painted of myself. I hated feeling like I was helping women out by giving them a good man when they didn't deserve one. It's funny how I feel like I can determine who deserves what. It's funny because it's true. Being egotistical is something I know I have to work on.

People always say they're going to work on something, but never do. It just sounds good. But since I didn't feel as though any of the women I encountered were deserving, I kept the good boyfriend traits to myself until I found the right one that was worthy. I rarely thought anyone was worth it. But who am I to be talking about being worth it, due to the tactics I've employed and behavior I continuously display?

Honestly, I'm not sure if I'm a good man. I go back and forth with this concept a lot. But I played the role well. I preyed on these types of women who couldn't differentiate between a good man and a poser. They were my favorite. They were the type of women that went through so much bullshit with men that brought nothing to the table which they carried over. It's kind of admirable when you think about it. I always had the visual of two people pulling up a chair and emptying out what they offered on the table and discussing whether the journey is worth taking. When you come across a woman that's been through so much shit that she's willing to carry the table to you, as well as what she offers, you have to praise that woman.

It's sick how I can think about praising a woman and taking advantage of her for the same things I praised her for. It's sad that I have to take advantage of them like this, but somebody has to do it. What type of man would I be if I gave the privilege of hurting her to another man? That's my job. I took pride in that. I wouldn't be able to live with myself if I gave up that opportunity.

NOTES

NOTES

STAGE 2

People always try to attribute my ideologies to the last woman that broke my heart. They believe without that incident, I wouldn't have the mindset I have now. And they're right. I should definitely credit that woman for who I am today.

Damn, I regret the way I mishandled my ex. You would love this woman. I just ran into her at the wrong time. I'm sure we can all relate to encountering someone you believed was perfect, but you weren't at the level you needed to be to enjoy that blessing. She deserves a better introduction.

When you're dealing with a good woman, all your senses heighten. You can smell better. You can breathe better. The only voice that matters is your woman's and your mother's. Food even taste better. You start trying new things just because you're in the great space. Your vision becomes clearer. You can grip your woman's waist a little tighter. It's amazing what a good woman could do. The more I think about it, a good woman just might be the cure for a lot of things. They keep a man safe and in the house. Every man knows there's no better feeling than laying up under your woman. So why risk having all these benefits, just to promote my own twisted agendas and keep my ego intact? I lost the woman of my life by trying to be the man of the moment. Damn, I miss her. I knew I should've remained me. I don't know why I ever switched up the formula. Now here I am.

NOTES

NOTES

STAGE 3

Maybe I do need to change. After losing this woman, you would think it's time for me to start appreciating a good woman for what she is and stop trying to alter her. I really wish I could. I wish it was that easy. But this is me. How can I just change what I worked so hard to continue to become? I was always a proponent of being pro me. I would rather the woman espouse my behaviors, opposed to switching up to accommodate them. Pride really fucks up a lot of potential blessings. But isn't that the case with everyone? Being pro them? Rarely do you come across an individual who would rather help structure the next person before they do for themselves. If you do happen to come across people like that, they are the ones who typically get taken advantage of. After everything I put women through, I couldn't afford for that to be me.

I'm stalling, I know. I'm still trying to find a way to appropriately introduce this woman. I just want to make sure I depict her correctly and do her justice while being blunt about everything. It's kind of impossible to do when feelings are involved, and the truth is demanded. I guess for feelings to be involved, that would mean we both ponder on this. I know she doesn't anymore and I'm alone on this one. I know she's out there making someone else happy. I'm more than certain someone else is out there appreciating her cooking and corny jokes. Appreciating how she makes your day better than it was just by hugging you. Honestly, I just wish our last memories were still in continuation and not confined to these last few pages. The journey is always better than the destination, I suppose. People always ask me if I still miss that woman. I'm here writing a book instead of talking to her, so, I guess it's apparent. I don't know if I miss her; I think I just miss learning from her. The women I dealt with prior to her never taught me anything. They were all victims. But not her. She taught me exactly what I didn't want to know. So maybe I just miss the thought of that, and not her. But here I go, lying again. I definitely miss conversing with her. I miss sharing ideas while lying in the same bed.

Some women are pure substance and others are pure beauty; she had both. It was a timeless type of beauty. The type of woman that looks better the longer you look at her. You don't find those types of faces often. I hate that even after departure, I still highlight this woman. I hate reflecting like this. I guess self-reflection is the best reflection. I honestly forgot the purpose of this passage. I just wish we didn't end like that.

I hate how vulnerable and sensitive I become when it comes to her. As I'm writing, it still amazes me. Why am I like this now? I was so accustomed to fixing women up, then being on my way. Life always finds a way to humble you. I always thought I was above this stage. I needed no humbling; I was what I needed to be. Thinking you're above the rehabilitation stage is hilarious to the Man upstairs; it has to be. Why the fuck do I still think about her the way I do? I should've saved these sentiments for my closing pages. I didn't even mention her name and you can see the vulnerability I exude and the influence she has on me. I don't think I'll ever mention her name; just for the purpose of keeping my sanity. I wish she was in my bed while I was writing this instead of in the saved images in my head.

I guess if she was in my bed, I wouldn't have anything to talk about. Even to this day, she's all I talk about. The women I entertain hate when I speak about her -- as expected. It's never direct, it's always subtle. Whenever I speak on what I want from a woman, I always find myself repeating everything she once did for, and to me. It's like when I think of the ideal woman, she's the paragon. It's fucked up that I try to equate every woman to her; as if she's the only good one out there. It's weird how men are always asking for something we once possessed. Sometimes, we know that our woman is all we have, and we still treat them any kind of way. Is that bad though? I think that has more to do with comfortability, than lack of appreciation. When you don't think your woman is going to leave, the security lowers. You aren't so adamant on trying to do the right thing all the time because departure never crosses your mind. Why would it? Why do women think we take them for granted? That's never the case. Part of the woman's job is to make her man comfortable, right? What happens when you get comfortable? You fall asleep. We're just reacting to the conditions that are placed upon us. So, if we fall asleep or get comfortable, it's due to your secureness.

It's due to the relaxed environment you created for us. When you're sleepy, your awareness lowers. Therefore, we don't take them for granted, we just never thought that we would ever depart. The issue arises when you put all this effort into building this place of comfort and we never settle in. You're placing pillows and comforters around him and he still finds a way to show discomfort, time after time, proving to you that you are not the remedy for his activeness. You're putting in all this hard work for nothing, ignoring all the men who would find it a pleasure to fall asleep in your lap while you're getting the bed ready. But whose fault is that? You can't force comfortability. I guess it's all about perspective.

We're supposed to be overly conscious all the time? That's bothersome. And if we're being real, women need to realize what they have as well and learn how to work with a man. You make too many mistakes, and here they go, accepting applications from other guys. You know how jobs always say they're accepting applications, but never hiring until something calls for someone to be replaced? I feel like that's exactly how it goes.

While you're working on yourself, they're in the back, scrolling through possible applicants to take your position. I don't care how many mistakes I make, don't depart from me. That's not what I signed up for. That's a sign of weakness to me. But here I go again, trying to justify why they should put up with my lack of productivity. I always told the women I dealt with that showing weakness or any sign of vulnerability was a good thing and that putting yourself in a position to get hurt due to the potential benefits of that risk was a strength. I think I just told them that to make them feel better about what I was planning to do to them. Honestly, that's the sole reason I told them that. I never really comprehended that notion, it just sounded good to me. Until now. But enough of that. The idea of seeming weak wasn't an attribute I was willing to take on. I guess being weak served its purpose because I couldn't think of an introduction until now

NOTES

NOTES

STAGE 4

Prior to my ex, I embraced this ideology I constructed that focuses on the two types of people as it pertains to relationships. The idea is that you're either a centerpiece or a missing piece. I want to thank the women I dealt with for this. I never give them enough credit for the way I think. I got a habit of leaving every ex behind whenever I entertain someone new, instead of embracing them for helping configure the man that I am today. If they did anything differently, I wouldn't be here. I mean, I would, just not in this capacity. I certainly wouldn't have a story to tell. I wonder if they still think about me in the same way I still think about my last girlfriend. I wonder what narrative they've constructed as it relates to us and our experiences. I'd love to get that perspective. It's weird because for a good amount of time I valued being a better ex than a boyfriend. It just meant more to me. I wanted my absence to mean more than my presence.

I valued being missed more than being had. I feel like people's appreciation for someone decreases when they finally have them. People love being complacent. Have you ever wanted something, but once you got it, you realized you appreciated it more from a distance? That shirt might look better on the display than on your back. I hated not being appreciated, so I opted to be missed. It seems selfish when I think about; disregarding how that impacts the person I'm entertaining at the moment. Being missed is just a feeling I'll never get tired of. Knowing that you cross someone's mind due to what you did in the past is the ultimate sign of control. I never knew how much control my exes had until I finished up that passage.

Do people randomly think about their ex? If you don't, that means you were never really invested when you were with them. I don't know if I can trust you if you were never invested. How could I trust you if you can completely forget about someone you potentially seen a future with? For the people that do relate, they can tell you that missing your ex is a dope experience. It shows you who you really are.

It definitely showed me. It was scary. You can't control that portrait; it is what it is. I hated seeing that side of me. I just wish I could apologize to all the women I used over this recent summer to get over my ex. If there's any consolation, it didn't work. Here I am going on tangents again. I hate when the thought of her interrupts what I'm doing right now. But whatever. I don't know why I find so much comfort with getting lost in thought. As it pertains to the missing and centerpiece concept, understanding it is extremely vital. Knowing who you are and what side you identify with is indicative on how your relationship will manifest.

The concept isn't difficult at all. The centerpiece is almost self-explanatory. The concept implies that you're the focal point and main attraction. For whatever reasons, people generally go out their way to get your attention and show interest in you. You don't have to do much to acquire it. People think you'll make them better by having you in their life. There's too much power in this role. If you aren't confident in how you conduct yourself, this position isn't for you. I always had a love-hate relationship with this position.

It's almost as if you're forced to be arrogant. I was already egotistical, so for people to display interest in me whether it derived from physical features, my affiliations, literacy level, personality or mental playground, it just boosted it. I felt as if I could do no wrong. And if the rare occasion occurred that I did, I wouldn't care. The attention would come to me from the next person anyway, so, why should I? If you're the catch, why worry about when someone leaves you for whatever reason they deemed appropriate? I used to envy women that knew they were well put together. They knew they looked good and men would risk it all to have their attention. I think I felt some type of way because they mastered the skilled better than I ever could. My strengths and valuable attributes derived from conversation. Women could garner attention just due to their visual. I had to work for it, they didn't. It's whatever though; it's not about them. The centerpiece appears to be a good role to side with, until you pay attention to what you become by embracing it. Along with being arrogant, you're work ethic decreases. I see why I needed my ex in my life. This isn't a behavior I should be content about employing.

Your work ethic decreases due to you being so prone to gathering people's attention, you tend to opt out of modifying yourself for the better. It's hard to get an idea of what's better for you when you're not used to accommodating to other people. This role is better suited for those who do not get impacted when other people's feelings get hurt as long as theirs are the priority.

Then you have the missing piece. The adapter is what I usually refer to it as. The missing piece might be the biggest role to play and arguably the most vital component. Basically, the role implies that you can deviate from your own agenda and ego, in order to complement someone else. You see the potential in others and feel as though you could leave the idea of being all about you and build with someone else with the intention of building a bond and a foundation. I applaud the individuals who make these decisions because I couldn't imagine doing so. I could never adapt like that. It wasn't ideal. What do I look like configuring myself to adjust to someone? I thought too highly of myself to change due to another individual. But I guess compromising plays a vital role when it comes to building with someone.

I wish someone had written about this perspective before I got to it. Someone probably already did, but I'm too arrogant in my way of thinking to even read it even if I were to come across that literature. I sometimes wonder what it's like to be dependent upon someone else for your happiness. But then again, here I go lying again. I knew exactly what it was like. I've witnessed it up close. I was responsible for creating these visuals. I used to break women down to their smallest component and have them dependent upon me for their happiness. I had fun with it, too. I hate how fucked up this sounds. Maybe break is not the correct term. Then again, maybe it is. I'm done using euphemisms. And I hate getting off topic.

But along with the centerpiece, there are flaws within this position as well. The biggest one is the possibility of getting replaced. When you go away from yourself with the hopes of building with another, you run the risk of getting rejected. A missing piece is just that -- A missing piece. No one enjoys rejection. That's scary; not being seen as good enough for someone isn't an idea most would want to digest. That's another reason why people might side with centerpiece position because that danger is eliminated.

How can you get rejected when people view you as a cardinal piece? Being replaced or disregarded doesn't sit well with anyone, obviously. Knowing that you deal with insecurity issues or just the thought of not being viewed as adequate, can make some people embrace the characteristics that come along with being a centerpiece. And that's where the dilemma lies. Adapting to a lifestyle that naturally isn't you because of the consequences of being you, will only lead to potential that isn't yours. Anything you accomplish after deviating from yourself will never satisfy you because you're living off potential you didn't intend on creating. There's nothing worse than living a life that isn't you because you're worried about how people will treat you. You see the crisis here? Knowing your role is vital because you cannot expect a healthy and prosperous relationship if you aren't comfortable with yourself. After losing out on so many good women, you would think that I would alter my behavior, lower my arrogance and adjust to a missing piece due to how things ultimately worked out for me in the past. But I didn't. And that's where I fucked up. Biggest loss in my life.

NOTES

NOTES

STAGE 5

I always wanted this woman. I saw her throughout campus multiple times, but never was afforded the opportunity to speak up. Of course, I'm lying again. I had plenty of opportunities, but never took the step. What is it about seeing a woman you want, but being hesitant to let it be known? I wish you could see her. Long hair, nice build with the most innocent face. The kind of face that needed no makeup, so you could lick it whenever you wanted. The kind of face you could take anywhere. An all-purpose face is what I called it. The type of woman with a face you could take to your neighborhood, museums, art galleries, etiquette dinners, picnics, your grandmother's house, and she'll fit right in. Every woman doesn't have that ability. No knock on the women who don't, but she just was in a category of her own. She was a quiet woman as well. You hear girls' names get thrown around on campus all the time, but never hers. She was different.

I never had a conversation with her, but her visual and exclusivity told it all. I could never get a hold of her, but I'd always see her around. Exclusivity will always determine your worth. No man or woman should be easily accessible.

So why didn't I approach this woman that I'm visually obsessed with and tell her that we're together whether she likes it or not? Because I didn't want to look as dumb as that sounded. Do women like that type of energy? Just approaching them and enlightening them on the plans you got for the two of you? Do they respect that? I wonder how women would react if you just walked up to them and said that you don't want to be with nobody but them. What would be their reaction? I should've tested that notion. I'm glad I didn't, though. I found out from a friend that she had a boyfriend; or whatever he was. I don't know why I expected this woman to be single. It never really works that way. That would've been too easy. It was expected. I would've questioned it if she were single. I probably wouldn't have even pursued it. I got a thing for already-involved women. They possess attributes that a man finds admirable, and I was always the one who wanted to figure out what made those women so special.

If you're single, it's for a reason, right? I'm tired of hearing "I don't have time for a relationship right now. I'm working on myself and focusing on my education". I'm real life tired of hearing that shit. Women need to find a new and better excuse for why they can't keep a man. It gets tiring. Then you have those who spew the idea that no man can handle them, which is the reason why they're single. As an adult, I don't know why women think it's cute to be handled. Maybe he's just not interested in you. Then again, due to my transgressions, maybe I'm not qualified to speak on this. Or maybe I'm the perfect suitor. I really hate looking at concepts and ideas from this pessimistic perspective. You can't convince me that someone wholeheartedly wants to be single. Everyone wants somebody's nerves to get on. That's just how it goes.

I caught wind that her and her boyfriend at the time were not in the happiest place. I feel like you can find anything out when it pertains to somebody you're interested in. It might just be from my experiences, but when I like somebody, it seems as though information about them just finds its way to me to me as well. You don't even be looking for it, and it just falls in your hands.

But I could just tell they weren't in a good place. Men just have this keen ability to sense when a woman isn't happy with their man. Shark sensing blood in the water type of thing. We see vulnerability and attack. You just have to be cautious of when you attack. The wrong timing could lead to you pushing someone back into the arms they were trying to escape.

The library and gym were her usual hangout spots. I was somewhat jealous because whenever I gathered whatever courage I could find just to say hi, her boyfriend would be there. I hated seeing them together. It didn't look right. Any woman I felt as though belonged with me, didn't look right with whoever they were with. The thing is, the person she was involved with was someone I knew. A cool dude, too. But you want what you want, right? If he and I were to stop communicating today, my life wouldn't change in the slightest. So what loyalty did I owe him? The most I ever seen them do was hug and hold small conversations. No kissing or any type of affection. That bothered me the most. I know all couples aren't big on public affection, but the way this woman was put together, there's no way you don't show her off.

If that was me… I feel like everyone had one of those "if that was me" statements. Everybody envisions wanting to be in a position they aren't in. How do you not grab her ass in public? Or kiss her nose or lick her face? I was big on being territorial. She could do better. I was her better. But I couldn't disrupt what he was doing to her. He was making my job easier. I could tell she wasn't progressing. Happiness shouldn't have a cap, and I felt like she been reached it. I just felt it. There's certain body language that's more telling than words. I could've made my presence known and made a friend out of her and progressed from there, but that would not have been fun. I had to let her create the separation herself. It was only a matter of time; so, I waited. I wouldn't have written this book if I didn't get what I wanted. Then again, that's probably the perfect reason to write it.

Over college break I received the news that she was single. Took long enough. The only problem I had to face was hoping no one got to her before I did. I had to pray her last boyfriend did the job I needed him to do. I needed him to be the reason her confidence lowered. I needed him to be the reason why she can't trust men anymore, so if I were to become her man, it would be harder for her to leave me because she's too invested. I needed her to be vulnerable. I needed her to be mine. If those fell into place, she would be my most valuable portrait.

New semester, new victim. At least that's how I assumed it would be. I made sure I was in the gym daily because I knew eventually I'd see her in there. I hated being in there day after day and not running into her. I missed so many assignments trying to keep up with this woman. If I miss assignments for you, you have to mean something. Clearly my priorities weren't in order. Or maybe they were. All I knew was that if missing assignments is what had to happen for me to find this woman, then so be it. Men are made to hunt. That's our natural instinct. We want something, we go get it, regardless of impediments or consequences.

When she eventually arrived at the gym, I eyed her down until we noticed each other. I hate when people stare me down, but I be quick to do it myself. We made eye contact and she walked over. Men always try and make it seem like they know what to say in every situation, but this one, I was stuttering before she even got me. The greeting wasn't all magical or special; it was quite simple. The simplest gesture -- a hug. Our prior crossings only involved a hand wave, so to be embraced with a physical act just made me want her even more. That's how all guys think. A woman gives them a hug and he automatically think she wants him. I would laugh if someone were telling me this narrative and believed a hug was a legitimate reason to court a woman. But whatever the case was, she embraced me. As she walked away after the hug, I looked and thought to myself, "her thick ass". You know how us men think and talk. I'm glad she didn't catch me looking. Honestly, I probably would've kept looking even if she had. If I could pull this one off, I knew I'd be the man. It took me forever to find this woman again, so I'd be foolish not to say anything else to her. Although the visual is pleasing, there's more to the criteria of being my woman. I need the conversation.

I need the support. I need attentiveness. I need you to find solutions for the bullshit I planned on putting in her life. Most importantly, I needed her to care. I needed all of that. I tested her to see the likelihood of her being willing to offer what I needed. I remember walking over to her grimacing. She asked what was wrong and I let her know I had a migraine. I always had a problem with them. Never knew where they derived from, but they just happened. I hate when my mental is impaired, but I love causing disruption in others. Hilarious, right? But the concern on her face was evident when I got to her. Of course she offered alternatives on how to get rid of it, but that wasn't what caught my attention. That wasn't what I was looking for. She actually made a conversation out of it, instead of just a suggestion. I'm big on conversation. Now that I'm thinking about it, I might just be blowing this whole scene out of proportion. Why am I internalizing every act she does as something greater than what it is? Maybe she didn't mean anything by it and was just being amiable. I feel like this whole book is compromised now. Maybe I'm in a fixed reality. But aren't we all? But I liked her, so she liked me too. That's my perspective and I don't care about the validity of it.

There at that moment, I could tell she wanted to speak to me as much as I wanted to speak with her. It was just something there. And I couldn't wait to find out.

I get annoyed with trying to find the proper way to walk you all into my heartbreak. This is probably my first time using that word. Not sure if I'm comfortable with it. Why do women tell you they aren't going anywhere, but as soon as the relationship encounter a few problems, they go somewhere? Is that just something they all say? Is that how they play their game? Make a man feel comfortable, then leave?

I caught her again at the library a few days later. She was sitting at the computer station doing whatever she was doing. It's funny because as soon as I walked into the library, I noticed a messy bun sticking out above the cubicle she was sitting at. My favorite hairstyle on a woman. I knew it was her. I got to brushing my hair and practicing what I'm going to say as soon as I got to her. I must've arrived at at least 30 different possible greetings. Why am I overthinking this as if we haven't spoken before? Time seemed to have been taking forever until I reached her. Probably because for the most part I was standing still. That speech we tell ourselves before we approach someone is always awkward. You always think of the first line, but never the follow up. I walked over to the messy bun to say something just to find out there was an empty seat next to her. Why didn't I consider this? The simplest thing. I'm laughing as I'm writing this because why am I considering every little detail. I clearly like this woman and care too much about how I come off to her. I don't like that. That whole caring thing wasn't something I was trying to get familiar with. But anyways. Since it took me forever to arrive to a greeting, I kind of felt obligated to sit down.

I was never this nervous before. I knew women too well. Too fucking well to be overthinking casual dialogue. I did this routine too often. I trapped women in their own psyche too often. I made good women turn great too often. This is what I do. I hate questioning my own capabilities. I wonder if she has a system she abides by as well. Imagine that. I knew there were more people of my kind, but I never thought I'd actually run into one of them; let alone it being a woman. I don't know if that was a compliment, or me being misogynistic. Maybe I'm just overthinking as usual.

I ended up just sitting down and saying hi. I was kind of disappointed that that's all I came up with. A grown ass man just saying hi is embarrassing; at least to me. There's more in my arsenal than just a hi. I'm much more critical of myself than she is. She didn't seem to complain or be bothered about how I approached her. I love a woman that accepts simplicity. It makes my job a little easier. I just wish I came up with something different.

That hi meant so much more than just hi. It meant be my girlfriend despite only talking to each other for about 20 minutes total since knowing each other. It meant don't be a challenge and allow me to infiltrate your way of thinking and alter it to my liking without you judging or ultimately leaving me. It meant be in my bed when I get home after leaving my night class. I hoped she understood what that hi really meant. It would definitely save me a lot of energy and effort. She said hi back. I wonder what the meaning behind her greeting. Maybe she's playing the game I'm playing. I'd be impressed if she was.

I didn't have any work to do, but I had to find a legitimate reason to be sitting here. Of course, she was the real reason. I should've pointed that out to her. I hate arriving to a better plan when the situation is already over. But I ended up pulling up pages from a book I was writing. She leaned over and asked what I was working on. Nosey ass woman. But I liked her. Therefore, she could be as nosey as she wanted to be. I informed her that I'm an aspiring writer and was finishing up a passage from my book.

I always had wild ideas and a weird way of thinking and planned to incorporate that into my notes. Some of the ideas are the same ones I mentioned in the intro. I contemplated about speaking to her about some of my ideas, but then it hit me. This is the perfect instrument to use to lure her in. I hate that it feels as though I was being sly and deceptive. It's probably because I was being sly and deceptive. She asked me what the nature of the book was, and I figured this would be the perfect time to test her. I just told her I'm working on this chapter entitled "No man wants a good woman to begin with". That wasn't the chapter I was constructing at all. I was actually writing about how there are no such thing as relationships. There are only temporary compromises and marriage. But that wasn't intriguing enough. Who cares about that? I wanted to see her react. I needed her to. I'm somewhat mad I started with a lie. But who doesn't lie? After I told her what I was working on she became more attentive. Her body position and facial expression changed as if she found what I was talking about interesting. It was all tactical on my end. I chose to add in the good woman part to see if she could identify with it.

People engage more when they feel as though something relates to them. Of course, she could relate. As soon as she gave off a reaction and participated in the conversation, I knew I had her attention. Finally.

We talked for a good amount of time. That surprised me. Usually when I speak with women, they don't know how to. Not in a literal sense, but as far as elaborating on abstract ideas and being able to get their point across appropriately; they weren't adept at doing so. We actually had a good conversation. I didn't want to leave, but I found an excuse for why I had to. I kind of wanted her to miss me a little bit. That's how I knew I was losing touch with reality. What did I do to believe that she would miss me? Not a damn thing. We spoke. This is probably what she does every day. Why would I think I'm special? But I noticed that she was intrigued, so why not take advantage of it? It was always best to leave first. It was just part of the system. Give her a reason to think about you; hopefully. Even though the conversation was great, I refused to ask for her number. Do men know that not asking for their number during the first few encounters aids in you getting her attention quicker?

She probably run into men all day trying to get her attention and asking for her number. She's more inclined to remember the guy who didn't ask, opposed to all the men that have. At least that's what I hoped. As I got up, I looked at her and could tell she wasn't ready for our conversation to end. Exactly what I hoped would happen. Step 1 completed.

I couldn't wait to tell my homies about me and my girlfriend's encounter. Yes, she's my girlfriend. Whether she was aware or not. We talked about everything. Probably because we were forced to because we lived together. I think that's a ritual with all guys to tell their friends about the girl they like. I walked in the house and they could tell I had something to say. I essentially told them I ran into her and we had a decent conversation. Your boys always find a way to clown you about being excited to see a woman. I had to play it cool, though. I explained to them that she was feeling me, and she was damn near begging me not to leave. You know how guys over exaggerate a situation. We laughed about the regular shit we talk about on the daily and I ended up walking to my room after.

I hate being alone in my room. My mind does its own thing. I start nitpicking at shit that's better off not being thought about. But it's just something that tells me that she's different. And on top of that, she seemed genuinely interested in me. I don't know why, though. I didn't give her enough of me to garner that type of interest. I did the bare minimum. She's making my job too easy. We spoke, and we laughed; that's it. I guess everything is contingent upon how they were treated in their last relationship. If they're so used to nothing, I guess receiving minimal effort would suffice. How long can someone get away with giving the bare minimum, but requesting the most from their partner? It's funny to ponder how the person who offers the least is the one that's most inclined to leave due to not having their needs met. Will she remain like this when I eventually show her the real me? I got a lot of shit in store for this woman. I couldn't wait to detach her from her friends and make her dependent upon me for company and laughs. I just want to bring her into my world to the point where she identifies with me more than herself. I go back and forth debating if I should continue to turn this woman into a project, or to make her my woman and forget about this game I'm playing.

The fact that I'm even over thinking this makes me question my intent. I'm the assertive one with the plan, so why the fuck am I overthinking this situation? I have to learn how to stop cursing. My mom raised me to have an eclectic vocabulary for a reason. I hope she's doing well. I just hope the next guy isn't plotting on my mother the same way I'm doing with this woman. My mother is too good of a woman to get hurt again. And here I am, trying to alter a woman who I feel has the same qualities as my mother. Men always find a way to mess a good thing up, and I know that's exactly what I'm doing. And I'm perfectly fine with that. Maybe this woman deserves to get hurt again. Why would I break the cycle? Why would I shield her from pain? I'd much rather add on, at least for the moment.

I camped out and caught her again at the library. She had to have known I deliberately did this. It happened too many times for it to be coincidental. Maybe she did the same thing. Maybe the conversation I have with myself, she has with her friends. On a campus filled with 15,000 students, it's going to be difficult to run into the same person multiple times in a week. We both had an unspoken understanding that this is where we meet. Smart woman. Made my job much easier. We had our deep and intellectual talks about nothing; as usual. I swear them talks meant the most. I forgot the content involved in our conversation, but I remember how it ended. She mentioned that it was funny how we always ended up seeing each other here. Is she fucking with me? Is she insinuating that I follow her around or something? I hate overthinking. The smile she put on her face seconds after saying that let me know she didn't actually think it was funny, but she actually enjoyed the idea of meeting up without making it complicated.

Little did she know, it's plenty of places I could've met her. For instance, her class that let out at noon next to the cafe. How she always kept her head on a swivel to see if she recognized a familiar face. Or I could've caught her while she walked to her early morning class. The morning was never my thing. I would've had to pass on that regardless. Or I could've popped up at her residence after receiving her address when I told a mutual friend that that I had her phone charger and needed to return it. But I just kept it simple and stuck to what was working and met her at the library. I wonder if she would've liked that.

"I'm sorry, I have to get going and return the car keys to my sister".

"You're going to leave before I make you mine before you know that you're mine? Why are you making this so difficult?"

Imagine me actually saying that aloud? What would that woman's reaction be? That would probably be the end of this book. I wouldn't have a story to tell. I wouldn't be damaged how I am now. Maybe I should've said that. That would've saved me from ending up here.

I offered to walk her home. She motioned that she lived a few minutes away from the library, as if I didn't already know. It looked like she was hesitant with deciding if she should allow me to walk with her. I packed my bag and put my jacket on, so she didn't really have a chance to make a decision. I don't know if she was used to aggressiveness, but I didn't really care. Sometimes you just gave to put them in a position to follow your lead. Apparently, it worked out.

As we were approaching her house, I was thinking of all types of goodbye gestures. I hated awkward situations. Do I walk her all the way to the door? Maybe I should stop short and let her know that I have to stop here because I'll be tempted to kiss her, and I didn't want to risk losing whatever this is. Damn, that would've been perfect. Maybe I'll save that for the next victim. It always seems as if you get the good ideas after the situation is over. I ended up just giving her a hug. A strong one. A deceiving one. A genuine one. So many feelings in one hug. She smelled like stability and soap. A weird combination, but a wanted one. I wasn't even trying to let this woman go. As I walked away I was tempted to do the cheesy look over the shoulder move.

I was always awkward with them type of things. Do I wink? Grown men don't wink. What shoulder do I look over? It seemed too complicated. Funny, nonetheless. Glad I didn't. I wonder what she thought about when she walked in her home. What do I do now? Continue my day? I feel as though my day doesn't even matter whenever I depart from this woman. I shouldn't have included that. There's many things I was probably better off keeping as a memory, rather placing in this book.

Back alone in my room. I can't do this to this woman. Things just flow too well. She listened too well. She cooked too well. She smelled too good. Maybe I should've gave this woman more of a voice. I got a habit of leaving out services this woman provided because, simply, she was too good to me. You have to start having conversation with yourself whenever you come across a good woman. The things we ask ourselves are always interesting. What's even more interesting, is arriving to a conclusion, but failing to implement the steps due to out our agenda. I don't know. The pressure a woman puts on a man to produce could intimidate anybody. What do I pick at? Do all men have this complex?

Do we all risk a good thing for our own benefit? I feel like we all do. We pray for a good woman, we get her, then lose her. Outside of pay periods when that direct deposit hits, this might be the best cycle to experience. It doesn't matter how long we ponder on how me mistreat women, as soon as encounter another quality female, we're repeating the cycle. But oh well.

Maybe I should force myself to change and just realize that not all women need rehabilitation. Why do I always feel the need to personalize women I'm already attracted to? Maybe I just want to be a part of something. I hate how cheesy that sounds. When something is natural, I guess there's no reasoning. A challenge is what I've been asking for. I wanted to encounter a woman that forced me to utilize different measures of control. I wanted a woman to put up a fight. I wanted to come across a woman that was smarter than me. Well, eventually, when I got older and was done with this game. So why complain now? This is the exact reason why I don't deal with good women. They make you work without even trying. In a way, you just feel obligated to. But there has to be something.

It's sick that I'm literally sitting in my room trying out different ways to discover her weak points. How weird is that? Why feel the need to self-sabotage a great situation, produced by a greater woman? But this is how we maneuvered. This is how I maneuver. I had a system that worked for me this long; I couldn't abandon it now. What type of man abandons his principles?

But then again, what does it 'working for me' actually mean? Writing this passage was the first time I ever asked myself this question. I really wish I wasn't the only one in my house. Usually my housemates are upstairs arguing about who has the most girls or who's the funniest in the house. But today, It's too quiet. Silence is never a good thing. Once you find comfort in distortion, you can never view silence the same. You begin to appreciate chaos. Chaos forces you to think. It forces you to adjust normal behavior and adapt to the current climate. I'll probably never answer that question of what my system working actually entails. I just choose not to. It's probably because I'm still thinking of a response.

This is a weird space for me. Very uncomfortable for some reason. I kind of want to end the book here, honestly. I be forgetting as the writer, I can do what I want. I don't know, I'll think about it some more.

I feel as though I gave the readers enough of me already. I introduced you to my world and walked you through my psyche. I know every book is supposed to end with a lesson or moral, but this just isn't one of those. I'm kind of disappointed that I couldn't be the man I needed to be for this woman. Well, I could've been, but being a good man is boring. Her in my bed is a much better visual than this pen and notepad. I guess forever does have an expiration date.

This is the me I hate. I don't recognize this person I've become. I alluded to the fact that I was arrogant in my way of thinking and I refuse for my motive to be altered. But what exactly is my motive with her? Why do I continue to question the process that I've followed for years for a woman I just met? The more I think about it, the more I want to end this book.

I wonder if women overthink as much as men do. Yeah, women talk a lot, but do they overthink? I wonder what she thinks about. I wonder if she confuses silence with distortion as well. I wonder if the idea of an us, overpowers her own agenda. I never understood the term 'us'. I don't know what it represents. I don't know if it's an idea I should embrace or neglect. I don't know. The more I write, the more I realize there's a lot that I don't know.

A few weeks had gone by now and I feel like I haven't accomplished anything; or at least something I could be proud of. Yes, we've established a liking for one another, but that wasn't enough for me. With my past women, I would have them yearning to speak to me, and be anxious to be around me because they all thought I was different. I hate the term 'different' now. Guys diluted that term by giving that "I'm different" speech to women, in hopes that it heightens their chances with them. As soon as you attempt to promote yourself and tell a woman you're different, she immediately checks you off the list of potentials. I hated that simple men ruin this for me.

But being different didn't really bother her. She didn't get riled up or feel any type of way when we weren't together. Or at least she didn't make it obvious. She was the calmest woman I ever encountered. I don't know how I feel about that.

Even after departure, I still find ways to glorify this woman. Maybe I just hate that I can't glorify her, turn around, and have her all in my face being annoying. Annoying girlfriends always seem to be the best ones. Or maybe I hate it because I can't thank God for her at night and be blessed to see her when I wake up. Reminiscing never did me any good. Why did she have to leave? Why she had to go and disrupt the vision? She was always the thesis of my prayers. Here I go again.

Nonetheless, she was the calmest and most relaxed woman I have ever met. She didn't dress too fancy and had a laid-back personality. How do you get a laid-back woman that isn't yours to react? You don't. Maybe I'm trying too hard and giving her too much praise. She's still just a female at the end of the day.

Maybe she isn't a good woman and just plays the role as well as I play a good man. Did you ever downplay a situation to make yourself feel better? I find myself doing that more often that I'd like. I have to find a way to get my confidence back. This bus ride to campus seemed the longest. Or maybe my mind was just moving faster than the bus that day. I wonder what I would've thought about if I had walked.

I sat at the computer pods in the library waiting for our usual meet up. I was more anxious to see her face than to develop my plan for when I see her. At this point, none of the women I entertained on the side held any relevance. Getting rid of all the people you entertain, just to focus on one, is a dangerous stage. I never felt as though one woman was above another. They were all equal to me, so for me to now want to make this adjustment is either a testament of my maturity, or weakness. I wouldn't even want to know the answer to that. But here I am, in the library, ignoring all calls and texts. I wonder what's taking her so long? This isn't like her. I know she isn't with another man. She can't be. She's not that stupid. I put in too much work for someone to treat me like I've treated women.

I have to cut that out. She isn't mine, yet. I got to the point where I actually started roaming the library looking for that messy bun and weird laugh. She couldn't abandon our unspoken agreement, right? You don't get me to this point just to play games with me. Why would someone want to do that? Especially if they aren't deserving of that. I walked back to my computer thinking I wasted my time coming. She's just like the rest. Making you comfortable with their presence, then taking advantage by coming around whenever they want. Showing interest and then leaving. I hate how familiar it sounds. As soon as I logged off my computer, she turns the corner, greets me with a smile and sits with me. "Where are you going?" she asked. Damn, I like this girl.

I know women hate when you bring up sex during conversation. I always wondered why though, as if they don't desire it as much as we do. I guess it makes sense - keeping it mature and classy. I get it. I figured I'd test this woman.

"When I look at you, I get a visual in my mind that produces 3 lanes. Friendship, sex and 20 plus"

I had to hurry up and explain before she reacted to me bringing up sex. I never had this conversation or thought before. I actually just came up with this when she pulled up a chair. I just needed a way to get her mind wandering. That's when there's the most vulnerability. It's something attractive about a woman's mind when it's open to exposure. It's not even taking advantage anymore; it's having fun with it now. Sometimes, I wish I hadn't shared certain ideas with the reader. I didn't need to put that in here. I constantly, unintentionally, paint myself as a villain and then expect empathy from others.

Nonetheless, I had to explain it to her. The overall gist of that conversation entailed that I want her in my life in all forms. I need her in my life in all forms. The sex part was obvious, but the 20 plus is what I really wanted her to focus on. I don't know which lane she ultimately envisioned us in, but I wanted us to indulge in them all. I noticed she became more attentive when I spoke this up. I guess women like when a man has a plan that goes beyond short term. And for a man to include her in his plans, is only a plus. I'm saying I guess as if I didn't already know this. I know what words catch the attention of women. I knew what body gestures to employ to garner a reaction. I was luring her right in. I sometimes think, if I was fully myself in all situations and was 100 percent honest, who would stay? I get zero every time I think about it. Looking back, I don't think I ever introduced my true self to a female. Every time I sit down and begin writing I try to answer the question of "Who am I?" Is it the conniving, cunning and manipulating self? Or is it the goofy personality, laughs, financial security and exclusivity I provide? It might've been beneficial to include this side of me more throughout this project. I don't know why I didn't initially.

Questioning my identity seems to be a theme throughout my writing. Why did it take encountering this woman for me to ask myself these questions? I was fine with myself before her arrival. It's crazy how sometimes it takes encountering someone to find yourself. I hate when I let old thoughts distract me from telling this story. Her story. I always find a way to make things about me.

I was waiting for a reaction from her, but she just sat, looked and listened. She was probably waiting for me to address that third lane. So was I. I assumed she was mentally vulnerable right now. I guess she didn't really have to be, I just need to stop bitching and execute.

"Then there's the last lane. I get so many visuals whenever I see you. My home, my room, my bed. My hand wrapped around your hair, kissing your neck, holding your waist".

I just stopped, looked down and smiled. Couldn't afford to finish and make myself look stupid if she ultimately wasn't interested in that picture.

I raised my head and looked at her for a response
and received a small one-sided smile and was told
to cut it out. Them 3 words 'cut it out' has so
many interpretations. If it's a woman you like,
that's used as a way to show liking, without being
too forward and establishing a small boundary. I
don't know if I failed or not at this moment. That's
an embarrassing way to go out if I did. But she
didn't leave, so I guess it wasn't that bad. Maybe
she didn't leave because she didn't want it to be
awkward and she already had it in her mind that
this would be the last conversation we had. I love
giving that 'this is the last time we'll meet up'
performance. You just sit there, nodding your
head to whatever they're saying, planning all the
ways to extract this person from your life. I
should've just keep it at the friendship and 20 plus
lane. What was I thinking taking that kind of risk
with a woman like her? But she's still here. For
whatever reason, she's still here. Whatever her
reason was for staying, I'll take it. It was almost
as if she did me a favor and pretended as if this
conversation never happened. We resumed to our
regular conversations and just laughed, relaxed
and pretended to do our homework. The usual.

As I continue writing this chapter, I realize I'm starting to regress. I probably been regressing way before that. I forgot all about the "plan" and became a guy that actually cared. I guess it's nothing wrong with caring for the woman you love. For the women you like; excuse me. But this isn't what I signed up for. I guess the women I encounter don't sign up for the manipulation and psychological damage I impose either. Things always seem to make sense when you look at it from another's perspective. I hate that I'm losing touch with myself. I guess until a man finds himself, he'll ruin every woman he encounters. The direction of this chapter definitely didn't go as planned. Maybe I just need to stop making plans, being as though they seem to be productive. I went from going in depth about being a psychological abuser to speaking about me and her. Us. Damn I miss us. I guess I do understand that term now.

I received a text the next day, so apparently, I didn't fuck it up. Reading this as someone who's looking over it for the first time, I'd be waiting for the excitement to present itself. Or maybe we've passed it already. I've lost touch in the processing of composing this. I get upset when I read books and it takes forever for it to grab my attention. I hope that's not the feeling this piece gives off. You've made it this far as a reader, so I guess I'm doing a good job. I just don't want to leave anything out. But how do you value one moment over another when they all contributed to the story? I guess I could expedite the process. You would only be aware of what I choose to enlighten you on. It's amazing how much power the author has. We can write whatever we want, and the audience has no choice but to take it for what it is. But then again, this story is worth it. She's worth it. Why do I care about how she's depicted so much?

NOTES

NOTES

STAGE 6

I finally got her to come over my house. It took me forever to accomplish this. I often had to remind myself that there's a plan. Now I find myself getting so excited about the idea of us, that I deviate from my own agenda at times. Maybe I need to reconstruct that centerpiece and missing piece concept again because this isn't me. Well maybe not reconstruct, but adjust my position. What if I am a missing piece? Seems like I'm forever gravitating towards her, trying to impress and prove that I am the one for her. If I adjust my position now, I would have to scrap this whole book. It would feel compromised. I can't switch identities like that. That's not authentic. Do you ever realize that you're wrong, but if someone can't prove that you are, then you're right? I'm glad I noticed this now, and not then. Who knows what ideologies I would've conjured up.

But anyways, we're all in the house relaxing and joking around. It's me, my housemates, this woman I'm obsessed with, and her sister. I think her sister was there, I don't remember. Crazy thing is, I don't remember any of it. I remember being there physically, but mentally I think I was somewhere else. I'm trying to find the importance in my announcing that, but I just can't find it. Why don't I remember? I want to say it's because I'm thinking of how to capitalize off of her being in my environment, but I'm not even sure of that. Why does forgetting a memory mean so much to me?

After some time of laughing with everybody, I made a gesture that she should follow me to my room. She stood right up and proceeded to follow me. For some reason I was surprised. That's all it took? a slight head nod pointing to the direction of my room? I wasn't going to complain about it.

"My room not clean or anything."
I let her know while walking down the steps that my room is a mess and she's about to see the real me.

"It's cool, I won't judge you."
I knew I liked this woman.

Finally, alone in my room with her. This is much better than being by myself. Everything seemed much calmer. My mind slowed down. I was breathing better. This isn't usual. I don't know if it was due to nervousness, me being uncomfortable, or if she provided that peace of freedom I needed from myself. Being able to escape yourself and have someone's aura put it back at ease for you is a dope feeling. We talked about so much, that I don't even know what we talked about. I'm going back and forth debating if I should tell you everything. As if I didn't already, right? I just wish I could fast forward to the moments I felt as though changed the dynamic of our relationship and my behavior as it relates to me imposing psychological damage. The moment that made me decide to be a better man. The moment when I knew I lost a good woman. I really do want to finish this scene, though, but I guess I do have to power to fast forward. Let's try it.

NOTES

NOTES

STAGE 7

I had to fuck up eventually. 15 outgoing calls and I don't know how many messages. This the shit I hate. Why the fuck is she ignoring me? She knows exactly how I get in these situations. You never know how annoying somebody is until they become yours. I know she didn't decide to give up on me before I had the chance to give up on her. That wasn't the plan at all. I was supposed to leave first, if anything. And If I was going to lose her, I would rather it be from a different reason than this. This event wasn't big enough. We can't depart under these conditions. I've been calling her phone all week and she has yet to respond or call back. This isn't like her at all. Then again, maybe this is her. Maybe she's fed up with my bullshit. And honestly, I wouldn't even be mad because I know I put her through a lot of shit she didn't sign up for. But I don't care how much we've been through, we shouldn't be here.

I got people walking up to me telling me that they knew eventually I would fumble her. The same people that were telling me that they were happy for us and it look like we complement each other well. Never think people are in support of what you and another built, especially if they don't have one of their own to celebrate. I had to learn that. They were the same people who were making an appearance saying some negative shit about our separation. I never knew this many people paid attention to our situation. It seemed as though they cared about her more than I did. You know whenever you're treating someone well and it's noticeable, everyone's going to hate and bring negative energy around. If I treated her well, I wouldn't be here, right?

I had another group of people approaching me telling me that they knew I would fuck up because she was way too good for me. Why did they feel the need to get that message across to me? What was the point? I usually don't let shit like that bother me, but once it became a common consensus that people believed it wouldn't work due to how good of a woman she is, it eventually got under my skin. The man's worth isn't evaluated when departure occurs?

It's just the women who get the benefit of the doubt? She's not this good ass woman everyone makes her out to be. Or the woman I made her out to be. I don't know if I'm saying that because I'm reliving the moment as I write, or if I really believe that. Departure always bring out the you that you tried to keep restrained.

Man, we were perfect. She did everything a woman was supposed to do. She was well versed in the kitchen, provided back rubs after class, didn't embarrass me when she went out, catered to my needs, and intellectually challenged me. The perfect woman. Or so I thought. I'll get back to that later. But at that time, she was all a man could ask for. And from what she told me, I was one of the best men she ever dealt with. I was always curious about receiving exactly what I ask for. Even though I pray to God for certain things, most of time, I hope he doesn't grant it fully. You have to be careful what you ask for because if you are granted with the things you prayed for, if you mishandle it, you can't blame anyone else but yourself. Knowing that you're completely responsible for mishandling a blessing weighs heavy on someone. I figured If I received partial what I asked for, me losing it wouldn't hurt as much.

All throughout the relationship we praised each other on what we brought to the table. It's weird because I thought no one could ever match me in that aspect. Every time I went in my bag to put out what I offered, she would match me. Every time. I pull out personality, she pulls out personality. I pull out culinary skills, she pulls out culinary skills. I pull out being a momma's boy, she pulls out being a daddy's girl. Same motion, same speed. Usually the person I'm dealing with would eventually run out of items while I'm still unpacking; but not her. She was with me every step of the way. That's scary. Dealing with somebody who can offer just as much as you. What leverage do you have?

Reflecting back, I could've handled our situation better. Why did I have to do that? I never met someone that paid so much attention to detail. I'm mad I ran into this woman at the time I did. Or maybe I'm mad because she was stronger than I thought she was. Nonetheless, I just feel as though we found each other too early. If I would've had at least one more girlfriend before her, I think we would've worked. She was at her peak and I was still climbing. It's crazy how a man's mind alters due to self-sabotaging.

This might seem a little weird, but after writing that last sentence, I took a good 2-3 weeks off from composing this book. I just needed to refresh my mind. Feelings started to reappear, and I realized I was giving this woman too much praise. Praise that she deserved, anyway. I hate reliving memories that I can't get back. Especially when the memories contributed to your new character. I changed a lot for this woman. I ate differently for this woman. I cut off all females for this woman. I gained a better vocabulary due to this woman. I became a better family man due to this woman. I learned to appreciate women, due to this woman. Here I go again. Those weeks off did nothing for me apparently. Or maybe it did. Reading over my last few passages, I can tell I wasn't all the way there mentally. I'm wrecking my brain for a woman that wants nothing to do with me. The value of something always increases when it leaves your hand and others have an opportunity to capitalize on it. Life is funny like that. That bike in your backyard that you rode a million times and rarely touch always looks more fun when you see someone else enjoying it. I'm glad I took that time off to refresh my psyche. I wonder what I would've thought of if I stayed in that moment and continued writing.

Man, we were almost perfect.

.

NOTES

NOTES

STAGE 8

Days later, still no response. Maybe I should've gotten the hint when she suggested that it might be beneficial if she were to take a step back from me and let her be alone. Be alone? What does that even mean? I really need to know. I think when women say that, that's inferring that mentally they left the relationship, and they're just waiting for their body to catch up. I came too far in my rehabilitation as a man to just let her walk. It has been a good couple of days since we spoke, so I guess her body is catching up to her thoughts. The thing is, I been sensed it. Conversation got shorter. The meals slowed down. Her concern for my whereabouts dissipated. The reality just never set in. But now that it has, it isn't sitting right with me.

To this day I still don't feel complete without that woman. Every woman I come across, I always find a way to measure them to her. Maybe I shouldn't do that, though. I'm sure there's more good women out there. But I also know for sure that there isn't another her out there. I guess I felt the same way when I met my previous girlfriends; like there wasn't any other woman that was better than mine. Writing that sentence down, I don't even believe it myself. As it pertains to my exes, I always knew I could do better, but I was comfortable where I was at. They let me be me without causing any type complication. Saying that I could've done better but I didn't doesn't sit well with me. I hate when people downplay somebody they used to care for, so I take that back. Because honestly, they aided in the creation of me. I hate getting off topic.

What I really hate more is when I speak about women that isn't her or my mother. I could never run out of words when it comes to them. It's a weird thing to get mad at now that I think about it. It's probably because every thought from here on out is past tense. Maybe she was put in my life to make me better for the next woman.

I'm just having a rough time dealing with the fact that I altered most of my mannerisms for her, just to end up without her. Can you tell I'm stressed? It's taking me way longer to write this book than it was supposed to. I'm all over the place and I can tell. I thought about revising this paragraph, but I feel as though this is too authentic. Too vulnerable. Too insecure. This is really how I feel about the situation, so why would I alter it for the benefit of the audience?

I ask myself everyday why did I mistreat her? She told me in the beginning of our relationship that the actions I eventually exhibited were going to ultimately cause her to walk away. But when things are going well, you never worry about what could go wrong. Why would you? You enjoy the moment for. What it is. I never imagined that I would exude that exact behavior she was referring to. There's so many different directions I want to take this chapter. Being in this space was never part of the plans.

If you're reading this, why did you leave me? I got so many questions for you. Never mind, I don't want to give that soliloquy. That wasn't the purpose of this. I know you probably tired of me speaking about this woman and this situation. I would be too if I were the reader. But it's like, have you ever had somebody give up on you as soon as you started getting things in your life together? Everything they complained about and wanted you to fix, you did, and they still left. That shit hurt, right? You start to regret transforming into this person because you did all that altering just to end up by yourself. I could've stayed the way I was. I could've been working on the next victim. Why did I switch up my system for this woman? I think I'm going to close this passage up early. I'm not liking the direction these last few passages. It's uncomfortable. It's funny because now I'm so willing to listen, compromise, understand the opposition viewpoint and work things out, opposed to the old me where I infiltrated women's psyche, manipulated and left whenever I wanted to. It's almost as if me and her switched roles. I knew that woman was smart.

I'm almost done talking about this. I took another week off before I began composing again. Every time I pick up my pen and pad it's seems as if my mind wants to stay on this topic. I'm really trying. I'm mentally scarred and it's evident. I wish I could provide a visual of what this feels like because I'm running out of words to describe my disappointment. It's almost like building a sand castle. Me and her constructed what seemed to be an unbreakable bond and had fun doing it. She did her part and I contributed and did mine. She found the building spot, I cleared the area of any debris. I piled the sand together, she sorted it out. The cohesion was perfect. What could deter us from building this bond? Besides me, of course. The process of building was exciting. Putting together pieces we didn't know we had until we sat down and worked together. Bouncing ideas off each other and making up for what the other one lacked. Then all of a sudden, an incident arrives, and a wave knocks down what we've built. You would think the only option is to rebuild and start over.

When I was a kid and my sand castle got wiped away by water, I was eager to reconstruct another one. Of course, I experienced some frustration, but the idea of building a better sand castle motivated me to get my hands dirty again. As I'm looking over at her, it just felt like she wasn't in the mood to start over. This is the first time I ever felt alone with her. Yeah, we endured a few conundrums, mostly due to me, but I was ready to put that behind us and move on. The agitator is always the one who wants to tell the victim how to respond to a situation they're responsible for. Although I didn't give her the best version of me, and the appropriate effort in the beginning of our relationship, I was ready to do it all over again because I thought she was worth it. I'm bringing sand over and gathering new tools to help restore what we once built. Why not try and build it again? If I had so much fun doing it the first time, what's the problem? I'm putting my hands in the sand, reforming the foundation, brainstorming on how to avoid that problem again by securing the weak spots. Then I look over my shoulder to see that she's just sitting there. No tools in hand or any drive to help me put what we had back together. It's almost as if she was waiting for this disruption in the sand.

I could tell this was her last straw. How could she just be sitting there? She forgot about the objective that quickly because of that little wave that knocked down what we established? She's walking away while I'm doing all the dirty work. I'm yelling, trying to tell her that we could build it again, we just have to adjust a few things. But it seems as though the more I called her back, the further she walked. I don't even want to speak on this anymore because there's no reason why she shouldn't be right next to me. I'm over it.

.

NOTES

NOTES

STAGE 9

I had to close the door. I wanted to jump right on her as soon as she sat down. I wonder how that would've turned out. She was already gorgeous, but for some reason she looked way better in my room. In my bed. Next to me. This is where she belonged. See, I jumped right into highlighting her once again. I have to work on limiting that. I could tell she was a little wary about this intimate setting. I finally stepped up and proposed that we should take whatever we have and make it more than what we're doing now. The library meetups and lunch outings were cool, but it wasn't enough for me. I'm sure she felt the same way. I hope she felt the same way. I told her dealing with me is a risk and a huge gamble.

I assured her that if she allows me to pioneer this, I'll make sure I'll never hurt her and put her in a position that would cause her to regret trusting me. Those words mean so much now. It's just some things you say in times like this because it sounds good. What was I supposed to say? Be my girlfriend so I can find a way to implement the attributes I want in a woman into you? Was I supposed to let her know that this is ultimately a game and she's just a pawn in my whole plan? Was I supposed to notify her of the pain I caused the last few girlfriends and that she was next? That wouldn't have been smart at all. So, I did what most guys do and made promises I knew I couldn't keep. And it worked. Surely she was hesitant with the idea of dealing with a man like me, but she knew there was something there. She was probably aware of something I had no idea of.

For some reason I felt like she was playing a game as well. Maybe not the same game as me, but it's something. I'd be foolish to believe that everything she says and does is all genuine. Every move I make, I'm meticulous and methodical, so it wouldn't be strange of me to believe that she might move in the same manner.

I wonder how many lies she told me in this sitting. It couldn't have been more than mine. This whole hurt before you get hurt mindset of mine has to go. I don't know why I'm making this a competition of who is playing what games and whose technique is more effective. But all mental games aside, this was a moment I've been wanting to experience for the last few weeks. This woman in my presence. The thought of me and her becoming an item. She was all for us working on building with each other. And so was I. I just had to make sure I didn't get caught. Even if she is playing this game with me, I have to take it for what it is and enjoy this game of wits. But for now, she's mine and I'm hers.

I always believed that the better the relationship is in the beginning, the quicker it'll end. It's crazy how much truth that holds.

NOTES

NOTES

STAGE 10

When your woman is crying, what are you supposed to do? I wish she cut that shit out. Why is she on the couch, crying and being all dramatic? I hate the sound of woman's cry when they are trying to speak as well. It's just a turn off for me. Why is she doing this? The bigger question I can ask myself is how could I just sit there and allow it? Of course, that's the question I ask after the fact, but during that moment I couldn't find a reason to console her. I didn't want to. What kind of man am I? I honestly forgot what caused this scene, but I know I handled it inadequately in her eyes. She's looking dead at me, crying, and I can't even make eye contact with her. You can just tell when your woman is eyeing you down in frustration. It was actually attractive to me, though. I like shit like that. I always wanted to see this side of her. I wanted to see the pain I caused her.

I needed to know how good of a job I was doing to create vulnerability within her. I'm kind of upset that it took this long for me to achieve this. This is a first. I have to work on expediting this process. I almost thought I lost my touch or something.

There's something about tears from your woman that makes you feel wanted. It's a feeling of appreciation that overwhelms you. I think every man should experience this. I know I was supposed to comfort her, but that isn't what I do. This is all part of the plan. I actually wanted to smile in the midst of her crying and yelling at me. It was a weird feeling that came upon me. This woman likes me. So why not keep it up? Although I move like this, I do see the wrong in my actions. I'm not completely oblivious to the fact. I know the risk I run of continuing this behavior. She could be venting to another man who could handle that situation more appropriately than me. I would hate for that to happen. Your woman's complaints could be another man's place of freedom. Some men live to fix the problems their woman faces while others tend to shy away from it. I feel like I'm attacking my own character right now.

I know I am. I learned that you can't be a man when it's convenient. Your lack of manhood always heightens her flaws. The things that she complains about wouldn't be as serious as you make it out to be if you were there to stand by your woman and handle your business. I wish I would've learned this before we departed. I'm sure the narrative of this book would've altered, and she'd be right here next to me. One minor adjustment could be the difference between being with the woman you love, or getting old and having a story to tell about that one woman you let get away.

What if that was my mom sitting there and her man was just watching her cry when he had the opportunity to heal whatever pain she was dealing with? I'd hurt any man that'll take on that behavior with my mom. So why do I exhibit this behavior with somebody's daughter?

I finally gathered enough heart to look her in her eyes. There was so much pain and emotion there. It gave off a feeling that said, "save me". I wish I knew how. I wish I wanted to. But I didn't. I honestly didn't know what to do. She seemed so hopeless and vulnerable. Why am I enjoying this? All this trust she put in me and here I am letting her down. I can tell she's thinking I'm just like the others and I transformed into the same guy I said I would never be. Why did I allow this to transpire? Writing this book made me hate myself. Why would I ever think this behavior was acceptable? Probably because I was able to get away with it for this long. No other woman challenged my actions or made me want to change, so why would I? But she's different. Was different. Whatever. I can't look this woman in the eyes any longer. For me to put her in this position in spite of everything she's done for me, was truly unfair. I can still hear her cries as I compose this sentence. I'm trying to move on from this scene, but that visual of my woman crying isn't a pleasurable one. But who's fault is that?

.

NOTES

NOTES

I REMEMBER

This woman did it all. I remember on my birthday she came to my house and brought over a plate of food filled with my favorites; homemade chicken tenders with homemade honey mustard sauce. I never had someone make homemade dipping sauce for me. The smallest things hold so much weight for some of us. We always applauded effort opposed to materialistic things. They could never amount in our eyes. She always catered to my needs. This was nothing new. It's crazy how we treat the women that stand by us as if they're disposable. Probably because everyone is. I made sure that the next person I'm involved with brought more to the table than the last. I'm a conscious disposer. But damn, I miss her. We have so many memories.

I remember sitting at home, thinking of ways to show my appreciation for everything she does for me. I know reading this I haven't announced any good that I did for this woman. You know how I got her, but aren't you curious to how I kept her for the amount of time that I did? I know I would be if I picked this book up. She always told me she loved flowers and food. I think food is the ultimate key to eventually be in a position to create vulnerability within a woman. Food just changes their whole attitude and behavior. Have you ever noticed that when your woman is fed she listens more and seems to be more at ease? Feeding her creates comfortability, which enables you to become a piece of their peace. Once you enter that domain, you're free to maneuver and impose any psychological damage you want without her putting a wall up. No one expects to be exploited when you become a part of their happy place. I shouldn't be speaking about this. This the same behavior that landed me in this position. If I don't participate in psychologically abusing women anymore, I figure I pass it down to men in training. Maybe I didn't rehabilitate. Sometimes, I do miss the old me. The me that didn't take in account of other people's feelings.

I remember one night I popped up at her house with pizza, wings and flowers. It was a simple gesture, but an appreciated one. The simple things mean so much to a woman that values effort. I never seen someone so excited for wings, pizza and flowers. And the funny thing is, I wanted to do this. This had nothing to do with my plan. I was pulling out all the stops. I was sending her flowers on the regular. Made sure another guy never had the opportunity to feed her. Whenever she went home to her parent's house, I made sure she knew she was always thought of and my main priority by sending her flowers and notes. Yeah, I'm hurt. I don't know if you can tell, but it's pain in every word formed. I can't even ask people to feel sorry for me due to how I treated women in the past. I was so comfortable with the old me. I was the one causing the disruption in my partner's life to promote my own agenda. I honestly don't know how to organize this paragraph. I just hate when my effort gets looked over as if I'm a regular guy.

I remember after classes we would arrange to do what couples do; eat and watch Netflix series' all night. The cohesion was beautiful. I remember we used to go the market and I'd joke around and pull my dick out in the aisle to make her mad. She always hated that, but I loved seeing her smile. I'm completely fine with making an ass out of myself if it promotes her happiness. I think most guys need to understand this concept. It isn't all about you when dealing with a good woman.

Men swear they're some type of genius or relationship guru after going through a situation, right? It's hilarious to me. But this concept is definitely one to take heed to. I found myself doing things I didn't want to do, but I knew it would instill happiness in her. So, why not do it? Do females really think we actually care about their day when we ask them about it? That's just a prerequisite step we take so that we can talk about what we really want to talk about, or just to show you some attention. We do that just to seem as though we're really interested, when in reality, we're just sitting there thinking about all the nasty things we want to do to you and what we want to eat later. Those things always seemed to be the same. I'm sure women do this as well.

Learning lessons when they are no longer applicable to your situation, hurts. Why are men so late when it comes to arriving to a solution to better the relationship? We wait until you finally leave us after giving us 28 different chances and we see you're better off without us. No visual is more devastating than seeing your woman be great with another man. That's when everything really hits us. We don't cooperate as well as we should while in the relationship because we never envision you leaving. If every man had the ability to get a hunch whenever our woman thought about the idea of leaving, we'd clean up our act up. I hate trying to justify our actions sometimes because we do a lot of dumb shit that we can't be absolved from. All we really have to do is behave. A man is going to act right with a woman he really wants to be with. If he misbehaves, it's because he doesn't want to be there. It's really that simple. The key is to get you a good woman and leave them hoes and any unnecessary drama alone. It isn't rocket science. I feel like I gained all this knowledge and figured how out how to handle situations better, just for the person I wanted to ultimately leave me. I guess I have to thank her because if it wasn't for her, I wouldn't have learned all this. I'm just upset that she can't reap the benefits of the man she helped create.

I remember we used to be over her house talking with her sister, having our usual conversation, and every time she made me mad or said something stupid we would play fight. I used to be fucking her up, too. It's a few times she caught me, and it hurt a little bit, but she'll never know that. Whenever she got too close I'd wrap my arms around her and grapple her down to the floor or bed. Seconds later, we'd be making up as if we weren't just fucking each other up. The play fighting itself isn't what brought me to this memory, it's the simplistic bonding and comfortability we displayed around each other and our friends. Having a woman that can play fight with you, kiss you, and then make you a meal all within the same hour, needs to be commended and admired. We could be ourselves around anyone. This isn't as easy as it seems. For us to be able to still have our interaction stay consistent regardless if we're at her home or mine is a difficult task. There was no awkwardness and trying to impress each other's company was never an issue. I miss them moments.

I remember when we first started talking and there was a party near campus I didn't want to attend but my friends made me. The party was crowded, so me and a few friends just stayed out in the hallway which was almost just as crowded. The hallway to the party always seems to be more exciting than the party itself. I was close to leaving but decided to stay there for just a few more minutes. I'm glad I did. As soon as I made up my mind to leave, I seen her thick ass walking towards me. She was smiling from the door, until she reached me. I wanted to smile as well, but you know I couldn't afford to do that. I had to keep my cool. She gave me the biggest hug as I caressed her. This woman still smelled like soap and stability. I forgot about what we talked about but that doesn't even matter. Her visual was enough. Some weeks later I caught her again at a house party. I was on the back porch wishing I was laid up with her and when I walked in the house, I saw her standing by the door with this fitted skirt on. I could tell she would much rather be in bed watching movies than being there. That's just a vibe I sensed as soon as I looked at her. She didn't want me to leave when I told her I was about to. Seemed as though everywhere I went, we always found a way to each other.

I remember those lazy days when all we did was eat turkey burgers and watch Prison Break. That was our show. I appreciated those chill nights way more than being out in public with people we didn't care about. The field can never amount to what you have at home. We had fun just laying down, cracking jokes and watching television. She always found a way to get her back rubbed, and I always found a way to get my ears massaged. Simplicity wins most of the time.

I remember having financial problems during one semester. She always reminded me that she would help me with whatever I needed. Why did I mishandle this woman? I never accepted the help due to being a man. I know for certain she understood that, but she still found a way to help. I could tell she noticed my situation was bothering me. I hated feeling as though I couldn't provide. I wasn't used to this role at all. In the beginning of our relationship, she never had to spend anything when she was with me. That's just how it goes when you're a man. Providing in all aspects was necessary; so, to get to a point where I'm incapable of handling those responsibilities, I didn't feel right. You know how weak of a man you feel like when your woman says she's hungry and you have no response for her? That shit will make you hate yourself and question whether you're good enough for her. Even though this only lasted for a short stint, it was enough to damage my pride. She still held it down for me though; for us. Every day, every other hour, she asked me if I was hungry with the intentions on cooking for me if I hadn't eaten. She found a way to contribute without impairing my pride.

Every man has to eat, and she made my road to financial stability that much easier by providing that service. I can't even call it a service because she found pleasure in doing it. Why is she built like this? And what is she doing dating a man like me? Looking back, I really appreciate that. There's something to say about a woman who caters to a man's appetite and wellbeing.

I remember a lot. I remember this woman ordering a box of my favorite candy that you can only get at limited facilities. The times we'd laugh about nothing because the presence of each other was enough to create happiness. I remember our shower and chill sessions. We washed up for 10 minutes and spent the next 30 minutes just standing up in the shower, talking about everything and just looking at each other. I remember them chick-fil-a dates we went on in the beginning of our relationship; how she always ordered humbly, but always found a way to take some of my fries. I remember taking a 5-hour drive just to see her and take her out to watch a movie and eat because I missed her presence after only being apart for only 2 weeks. I remember I had a bunch of schoolwork to complete by a certain day and she helped me by composing a whole paper for me. I remember waking up and her being the first person I see. I remember going to the mirror to brush my teeth and her being right next to me, mocking every face I made. I remember her smile. I remember that ugly but cute face she makes when she laughs. I remember that ugly sound that came with her laugh.

I remember them days we argued but made up the next day because we were bigger than any complication we came across. I remember her telling me she's all for me. I remember me telling her I'm all for her. I remember the day I told her to trust me and that I'll always be there for her. I remember the day I didn't keep my word about being there for her. I remember the day I lost her trust.

Them "I remembers" meant a lot. They still do. So how did I allow us to end up here? I look back up just to see that the tears and pain are still in her eyes. I'm not providing any of that security I promised her. Everything we've been through, and I'm sitting here treating her as if she's nobody.

NOTES

NOTES

STAGE 11

I wanted to call her after finishing that chapter. I feel like there's a lot to be said that I couldn't communicate properly back then. This clearly isn't that same me you read about in the beginning. I did a lot of fucked up shit during our relationship and expected her to stay. Well not a lot, but enough. I wasn't as mature as I thought I was back then. I'm hoping the men can relate. When you're dealing with a woman that's more mature and can handle situations more efficiently than you, you get intimidated. Not intimidated as in you're scared, but in the sense that you have to work extra hard to prove that you're her equal. Pride is a motherfucker. We try so hard to catch up and cover up our flaws to prove we belong, that we make the divide even wider between us and our woman. With men being so arrogant and unresponsive to criticism, we don't see when our woman is giving us a platform to help us grow.

We feel as though this is a journey that we have to endure on our own. And that's where we go wrong; thinking that the road to progression doesn't involve the woman you're lying in bed with every night. Thinking it doesn't involve the woman that genuinely cares about your wellbeing. Thinking it doesn't involve the woman that you're doing this growing for in the first place. It starts and ends with them. That's how relationships become unhealthy; being too arrogant in your ways and ignoring your woman due to you trying to work on your maturity. The narrative that women are supposed to stay in unhealthy relationships for the sake of allowing a man to mature needs to cease.

Prior to my ex, I would've never thought I could establish feelings for a woman. Clearly there's the obvious stage of liking someone, but I never thought I'd arrive to a point where I couldn't imagine seeing myself without somebody. I never put that much faith and hope into someone. Not only did she bring feelings out I didn't know I had, she made me want to display them. Too bad I never did. I should've allowed myself to be a victim of her vision.

She let it be known verbally on multiple occasions that she's glad to have me and sees something different in me. Not only did she verbalize it, her actions backed up those sentiments. So why couldn't I do my part and give her reassurance that I'm on her side as well? Although I spewed similar sentiments, my actions were sometimes inconsistent. It doesn't matter what you say to a woman, if your actions don't follow up your speech, everything you say is taken with caution. False hope never works with a good woman because words could never amount to actions with them. Actions provide reassurance. And the thing is, that's all women want. They want you to rub their ass and give reassurance. I swear everything seems more sensible after departure. I'm still stuck on why I didn't provide that stability for her after all she's done for me.

.

NOTES

NOTES

COMPLICATED SIMPLICITIES

If I could paint a visual, it would be me,
locked down in a clear box. The box symbolizing
me not leaving my comfort zone and being
content with how I behave. Although I'm stuck in
this box, I can see everything on the outside. As I
look ahead, I see her trying to get this box open.
She's trying every technique. She goes from using
brute force, to a crowbar, a hammer and then to
prying it open with her bare hands. All while I'm
just sitting there watching. I could help, but I
chose not to. I wanted to see how much she really
wanted this. Usually this is the role of the man
trying to display his liking for a woman, but
somehow, she ended up in this role instead of me.
Not somehow because I know I purposely put her
in this position.

Looking back, I should've been in that box applying the same pressure as her. What was I doing just watching her exhaust all that energy while I did nothing? I wonder how I would feel if we switched roles. I wonder how long I would try and break this seal before I eventually gave up on her. Now that I think about it, I don't think I would waste my energy doing so. Why should I have to work that hard to get you to take a chance with me? I could never be outside that box trying to help someone get out. If me being there isn't enough, I don't need to be there. Why do that when I could entertain someone else who wouldn't make things so difficult? I'm glad she didn't think that way.

Nonetheless, it was admirable watching her put all that effort into trying to get me to open up to her. While she's doing that, I'm looking through the clear box and seeing what's outside of it. I see sightings of comfort, continuity, support, affection, dedication, catering, persistence and the willingness to love a man with no direction. She's offering all of this and all I have to do is help her open this box. She never gave up, though.

You would think that exerting this much energy into a project that isn't giving you the benefits you need to receive would deter some people. But not her.

I wish I could've found some motivation to help this woman. She was putting her all into it. Looking fine as ever putting them little muscles to use. I loved that visual of her struggling to get me to appreciate her. I see the emotion in her eyes. I see the tears; the struggles and the eye contact she makes with me that says "help me." I see it all. And I enjoyed it all. I got her exactly where I wanted her; vulnerable and dependent on me for her happiness and satisfaction. That must be a decent feeling; to have someone dependent upon you for their happiness. I love the position that dependency enabled me to be in.

Through all this admiration, I see that she'd made progress. As soon as she does open the box slightly, she looks over at me waiting for me to join in and appreciate what she has done. Still, I remain there. It took her long enough. All that time it took, and the waiting she had me do, made it hard for me to want to help her. I got bored sitting in there waiting.

But honestly, I never came to the conclusion that she would ever break this barrier. I went into this relationship knowing that nothing could be done to change my behavior. She lost the battle before she could prove her worthiness. Looking back, I regret it. But here at this moment, this visual aligned perfectly with how I envisioned it all along. That's fucked up; putting someone in a position that doesn't produce a positive outcome no matter what they do, due to you worrying about satisfying your own needs. I was wasting this woman's time. She made me value mine. She could've been with another man that wouldn't even allow her to get her hands dirty by putting her hands on this box, instead of dealing with a man like me. But another man wasn't in this position. I was.

Honestly, I think part of this behavior derived from back when I was making arrangements for her to be my woman when she was involved with her boyfriend at the time. He didn't have a big enough of an impact on her; at least that's what I've been told and seen for myself. Her caring level wasn't what it needed to be, and I knew that. She was still too innocent. She still had a lot of hidden potential. I brought that out of her. Where's my fucking credit? Do people not see that this is a skill? Art in its purest form. But then again, what I do isn't for the people to recognize. The only people who reap the benefits are the victims. I hate talking about this.

Have you ever doubted somebody's ability to overcome some complexity and then regretted it immediately after because they succeeded and now you're in a position where you have to respond? I look up and see that's she's exhausted. She sweated out her hair, her fingers bleeding, and she's just lying on the ground. She did it. I never imagined this box being exposed. Better yet, I never envisioned myself being exposed. There's something to say about a woman who risks embarrassment due to the benefits that could come from the efforts they put in. I still get visuals in my head of her crying on my couch as I write this. It's too vivid. I can hear the cries, the breaths in between her sighs, the embarrassment in her eyes. Why didn't I just walk out of this box? She's sitting there, just waiting. I'm sitting there, just staring. The conversation we had with our eyes spoke volumes. I wish I could capture that moment and eye dialogue in words. As soon as she started to gather her things and walk away, I reached out and grabbed her arm.

NOTES

NOTES

REALITY

I never thought I'd be waking up to this woman again. Or maybe I never thought I would get away with my behavior and have her forgive me. Damn, I love this woman. I have to put this pen down. I wish I could elaborate more, but these memories are all I have so it's probably better off if I keep it to myself. I know I put this woman through obstacles she didn't deserve. What kind of man does that? I know I wasn't much, but I was hers. In that moment, you never really stop and think that one day in life, this moment will just be a thought of what was.

.

"To: My Nigga,

Thank you for treating me like a princess. I know you have a lot of responsibilities, but you always make time for me. I appreciate you and the effect you have had on me.

Love: Your pain in the ass"

-   A great woman

Jameel Watson

.   .

Jameel Watson

66596457R00099

Made in the USA
Middletown, DE
07 September 2019